Lethargic vigilance

Eduard Harents

ISBN: 978-81-19228-59-1

First Edition: 2023
Rs. 200/-

Rochak Publishing
HIG 45 Kaushambi Kunj, Kalindipuram
Allahabad - 211011 (U.P.) India
http://www.cyberwit.net
Tel: +(91) 9415091004
E-mail: info@cyberwit.net

Contents

* * *

Van Gogh got rid of his ear,
because he didn't need it:
he had already heard the Genius.

Al-Ma'arri actually could see so much,
that eyes were
no longer so important.

Charents had no grave,
because
he is not dead yet.

I greet people with my left hand,
because with my right hand
I have already greeted God…

Translated from Armenian by ***Artur Avagyan***

---

* Charents – **Yeghishe Charents** (Armenian: Եղիշե Չարենց, romanized: *Yeghishe Ch'arents'*; March 13, 1897 – November 27, 1937) was an Armenian poet, writer and public activist. Charents' literary subject matter ranged from his experiences in the First World War, the Russian Revolution, and frequently Armenia and Armenians. He is recognized as "the main poet of the 20th century" in Armenia.

Still life

At midnight the Shia kids dream of morning, harvest,
while the hail of the Sunni-Saudi cyclone
reaps its neon harvest
in the gardens of ritual fate of Aleppo.
The cold is sieving Ash Thursday
over the city's Friday-white skin.
Hamito-Semitic berry-consonants
explode in the throat of the dawn.
Through the cough, the slim smoke of narghile urges,
where a young geisha's peach-like eyes mature
(those are unsurpassable almonds from Hiroshima).
Pages of Sharia are falling down from the trees,
like leaves, between the lines of which
huge palms collapse
from the solstitial and sun-averted Promised Land.
They herald from the ferries of the Dead Sea
about velvet pillows, like the Turkish language,
the German sonorants-pins of which
prick with silverberries the bellies of the pregnant women…
The blind travel toward the pomegranate taste,
the orphans play marbles with the grenades.
Red milk hisses from the covertly matured nipples of the Muslim maidens,
along the pure rivers of which
white cradles flow forwards Deir ez-Zor…

Love

Trough the 30 dawns of my life,
from flower to flower,
leaving all my sins aside,
by the time I arrived,
she had already left,
leaving the Supper table behind…

And I
laughed the words
inwards until yesterday
like
psychotropic fish…

It turned out 33 was too many…

* * *

In all my places of absence
I sow my reticence
from you…

Yet who punctuated
among the scents of my word?

Absolute scars,
inside my forehead of a vigil dream…

Whenever you wish to translate
my bloods,
collect Job's stones
from my poems…

Those are secret cells
of your Son's
round-scripted sorrow…

Ochre in C major

Up the unhurried roots of the night,
in circular movements approaches
the engagement of the dawn,
which divides throughout
the flower's triangular pistil,
where salt eats up the skeleton of fish
in the fisherman's liver…

From among the sorrow
of dark waters dies
the subconscious of
Good Fridays.

In front of the doors
I strip myself naked of myself
and from my voice remains

a signature in Jesus' style
on the dew of the dawn…

Translated from Armenian by ***Anna Talalyan***

Yearning

The shadow of color
is scaling
the scars of day;
walking the serenity
of an encountered dream…

The flower is the secret
of pain;
an introspective smile.
The scion names the sin.

Beyond personal bandages
of prayer,
the self-denial of a tree
is as much bright
as warm are the hands
of night.

I am freezing… your name.

* * *

I know, I will wake up someday
from the mystical dinner,
will wear my father's
damaged footsteps
as little pockets
filled with immeasurable love…
Can my days " I wonder "
scale that much unbearable
lightness?

* * *

My name
is a stone in God's dream,
with ornamental carvings
of askew mirrors.
Through the rib bones
    of light
my father's cataract
is tinkling on my tongue.

* * *

After so much pious,
loveless nights,
I have no idea from which
    muscle of time,
but storms are ringing from myself
apparently sweeping away all my
morns, which
remained punched like that
up till now
like the shoes
of a gold medalist student…

Interesting:
that much rich, so sonorous,
to which gates
will my evening – one day –
tinkle?

Odyssey

We ate poetry,
smoked silence
with a cup of coffee,
we got away from death
    chewing colors,
but still we are gazing
at the word…

* * *

I love you, daddy,
because the roses
of your fate's meadow
are prickling my feet.

My lines are red rivers
down the thorns
flooding the roots
of my love…

Translated from Armenian by ***Harout Vartanian***

* * *

Life lives me with all my details,
and I turn around it
as a color of another brush.
My canvases have holes in them
as a Japanese coin,
through which one by one
all my loves free themselves
from me, always outwards
their parting
ringing about my wonderful loss…
And my claps
weigh heavier than I do.
So I have collected them
in my hand
as smashed paper money
and keep them
for the last – the death
to revamp its masks,
that will be hole one day,
as my canvases are.
And I'll ring out forever,
and life will go on to live me
with all my details…

Translated from Armenian by ***Vanuhi Alabekyan***

* * *

I am plucking now
the eyelashes of silence one by one
to mend my prayer,
which has been torn by nuances of word…
Now the nuance is more than the voice…
And now I enter
the church of Hope barefooted,
so that my steps will not paint voices on my fortune.
How many footprints have been split apart by whispers…
While my footprint
is my prayer of love,
which never ends,
as it never colors itself in words…
And now
the main color is the truth,
that love is the poem of the feeling…
That muses don't turn into women…

Although

The day is wet like a door,
by which
from me I enter into you -
my back turned against the noise,
as if when leaving the church.

The bowls of hope,- drunk by me -
stumble behind my flower,
and mote by mote
my bright back bows down
on the impersonal suffixes of your threshold…

And you, suddenly…
not looking, you see me,
that I collapse on you
and you have no which were
to surround my back…

Your arms have remained in the church -
to pray
with the subjunctive of hugging me…

* * *

Like fever,
the moon angle is complex
and bright…

The night is a river
blindly entwined from the nuance of the star…

The rose-braid sky is fractioning –
hung on the plaits,
like shudder
of God output from the lip…

Exquisite catatonia – with seven birds…

The times are the pollination of your bird
in my flower's dream…

You haven't come
into my heart again
as you have locked it with the letter of your name…

The tear is the door
under the angle of my bird…

I am inside of you,
and you're not from you…

* * *

Red,
    red,
        among your red oaths
the colors of the angels
are reluctantly raining;
the rain is punctuating squalls
on my soul's pavement,
which you're
breathing
            now -
                    as a crock-crow…

* * *

This poem,
which calls me father,
which eyes are full of endless laughters,
it chimes so in my moments of sadness,
like my smile
is it's lost toy…
It always wins in every play,
is telling about it's beloved girls,
and before sleeping
he orders,
me to tell the tales of
my childhood…
And me like a foolish autumn
crumble before my miracle…
And taken the yells of my child in my palms
I am whispering:
– You self are the fairytale dotty.–
… And of the delight,
that I can't remember
any fairy-tale in no way,
he is laughing at me
all the night -
till dawn…
Then -
the mirth jingle kept between eyelids -
enters to a nap tabernacle.
If my song is sleeping,- only with open eyes…

* * *

Let's get acquainted.
My surname is Love,
and my name - Kiss.
I've eyes green
and blue moon
and universe-vein –
with mornlight blood.
And so I'm born on the beginning
of Eternal century –
on the Instant month
of the Joyous year –
on the night of Secret of the
Mythical day –
on the love of Needy and Return,
with the body of the mystery…
Well, I'll tell you one thing more,
I love those,
whose name is Love,
and surname – Kiss…
Let's get acquainted.

* * *

On that red day
yet the pagan grandmothers of my muse,
with a closed secret ballot,
had decided that
after nine months
under the songs of Bakunts' pheasants
should be born the poet of their granddaughter.
And as they were godfearing,
therefore decided-
the last apple of Heaven's trees,
which wasn't given to any physician's windfall-
to hide it under my mother's lap with care...

In August of 1981-
my father was distilling mulberry vodka...

* Bakunts – **Aksel (Axel) Bakunts** (Armenian: Ակսել Բակունց, Alexander Stepani Tevosyan; June 25 [O.S. June 13], 1899 – July 8, 1937) was an Armenian prose writer, film-writer, translator and public activist. A colleague and friend of Yeghishe Charents, Bakunts was a member of the former's Armenian Association of Proletarian Writers. Bakunts fell victim to the Stalinist terror and was accused of various crimes including alienation from socialist society. He was arrested in 1936 and is believed to have been shot after a twenty-five-minute trial in 1937.

* * *

Dreams… Dreams are the wings of the soul,
that fly upper than the soul.

Biography is only a shade of the destiny:
it appears when the lights are burned.

Confessions are the best plays of forgiveness,
which lasted longer than the play.

And… the worries are the children of the homecomings
who are born… before the parent…

* * *

There are such women,
who
after losing hymen
are staying more than virgins…
Such women are
all candles…

Translated from Armenian by ***Herminée Arshakyan***

Dilemma

In the mirrors
of tides
they always sit
in the same pose…

The lady who plays the violin
and the pregnant woman…

* * *

The bird was moving restlessly
around its cage:
there it had left its dream of freedom…

* * *

I am a poet
and poor:
I take care of the angels…

* * *

While I'm thinking my tree,
the love keeps Lent.
Green birds in my poem…

Photosynthesis of Narcissus on the back-ground of litmus

Before going to bed
the angels read
Narekatsi*
to God.

Lethargic vigilance…

---

* Narekatsi – **Grigor Narekatsi** (Gregory of Narek; 951 – 1003) was an Armenian monk, poet, mystical philosopher, theologian and saint of the Armenian Apostolic Church and Catholic Church, born into a family of writers. Based in the monastery of Narek (Narekavank), he was "Armenia's first great poet". He is the au-thor of a mystical interpretation on the *Song of Songs* and numer-ous poetic writings. His Book of Prayers, also known as "Book of Lamentations", a long mystical poem in 95 sections written around 977, has been translated into many languages. The book, the work of his mature years, remains one of the definitive pieces of Arme-nian literature. He was declared a Doctor of the Church by Pope Francis in 2015.

* * *

The tear is what believes the most
in God
It pays a visit always to the church of Hope.

* * *

In the destiny of the angels
the dreams of the fetus
are growing cellos.

Uterine jazz…

* * *

Death is the movement of travel.
It is a pity I will die-
never-
so I study the paradise of color
on hell's gates...

* * *

The poet's mother's labor is
always
left unfinished...
And all the time
it finishes with his every
next
creation.

* * * (Haiku)

Life is a narcissus
in the mirror of war.
A ruined face of fragrance.

Translated from Armenian by ***Shushan Melik-Adamyan***

Sanscri(p)t(um)

Your silence -
the only immature pistil of your mortality.
One day it will bloom...

And you will gain immortality.

* * *

After each incomplete moon,
until before every full moon,
splash after splash on my breath
grow upside down,
Father, you see:
dark white rose thorns -
your unlived days.

* * *

Your shadow
has no name…

But your name is
always leafy.

Whos nationality are you from?..

* * *

Who you running away
from the stones,
does not know
the right word…

to whom you give
your words,
throws stones
at you…

* * *

I speak in you,
your angel
rings in my palm.

You are dying
from me.
I am resurrected.

who has hole pockets -
full of impossible roses?

* * *

We are all lotuses -
grown from the gods…

We are nourished
by mixture's wonder of
life and death.

Divine sigh…

Translated from Armenian by ***Tatev Grigoryan***

* * * (Haiku)

From dream of those,
who fell asleep, a sprout of cherry
has sprung in the ground.

Translated from Armenian by ***Sophia Chilingaryan***

* * *

The day's like orange bites
as the hips of a lady...

Little slum dogs parched out
will die
leaking their own veins.

Angel's pillow will get sweated
under the skin of their own dream.

Out of a calyx of a broken word
Light bubbles
will toll...

* * *

It was your death,
that you loved in me,
o, girl,-
so that you live, and I die.

But from within my death
lose my name,-
so that you do not die,
when I become death!

Translated from Armenian by ***Maneh Kocharyan***

Cairo

You are a woman-city with pyramid breasts,
leaned to the backbone of the millenniums.

You are a woman with arched cupola,
like a Muslim afternoon;
you are a woman with niqab,
like voice of Ibn al-Qulsum;
you dream on looking into broken mirror of millennium,
like last
hieroglyph.

You are a city having charms,
like Arabic round nights.
And you smile as big as your Egyptian pyramids,
dark and marked.

You plant a Fairuz-flower
within every day after noon,
like a Hookah smoke,
in your thin throat
as number and order of Koran's pages,
like a Lullaby song.

You do not have the right, to have a short skirt on,
and go out, or to walk at home.
And especially lie on the side-bones of the centuries,
looking at the heaven.

You do not have the right,
but, even, you do not care,
that the wind of centuries
gives the birth
under your short skirt,-
from your moles of side.

You are so calm,
quiet like mummies,
that is going to give a blood for DNA
in the evenings…

Even, you are not shamed for your legs
white and blue.
For your legs, that lose their strength cause of wine, forever
like a snake - girl in that papyrus.

Jubran Khalil Jubran

An Arabic heart of rococo style,
every day,
after each ninth wave of crazy sun,
makes Lebanese moles
on the heart of giant New York.

B Flat

My mother's tear like a flower
drop from the mind of God.
Hemiparesis on the right side,
you are the woman without bra…
You are the night of my green-faith.
Take my left hand as a bra for your breast -
not to be shamed,
not to be afraid,
not to lose your milk cause of cold!
Take my left hand as a bra for your breast
to protect it from the coldness!
I don't want my mother's tear to shiver.
Therefore, let my mother's sadness
drop on my hand.
As it draws flower-moles on the bras you don't have.
My mother's tear like a flower
drop from the mind of God.

Translated from Armenian by ***Lusine Harutyunyan***

* * *

Summers are crumbling flushing,
as Rodin's «Danaide's» membranes of brain…

Autumns are weary untidy from fate,
out from their hue -
as painter's bra - splitted in barocco style…

Winters are self-refute pistils'
pallid prolongation
from green dreams of angels …

But still I'm the spring
of unrequited love…

* * *

Under the window of poetry
from each end till the beginning of the century
I lavish serenades drunk…
And till around me membranes chewing
prostitute times,
for captivating my heart,
are changing the hues of
their die for barren underclothing,-
my beloved color in the world
Is the poetry…

Translated from Armenian by ***Ani M. Hakobyan***

* * *

We are fragile dreams
in the curtain's tear.

Through each other,
trembling each other from within
the words throw us themselves
as a discs…

And immortals are those,
who will catch the discs
of our death…

Translated from Armenian by ***Hermine Araqelyan***

The eleventh commandment

When you let Love go from your hand,
give a clap to
your soul's *«weakness»*.

And to forgiveness of the light that flew
from your eaves
give a clap -
with palm to your cheek
from which you tore the flute of aroma.
Give a clap to the flute…

One hand gives a clap too…

Accusative Sunday

The night's roses are white
like Hebrew language.

I watered the lost prayers of crescent.

In the morning… the sense of smell
was Armenian
like red…

Prayer

The God sees you in his dream.
The conversation between mice and bird…

Mary Magdalene

Give back the stones
that I threw on you:
there are vacant holes in the walls of
my room…

* * *

Today,
more than ever,
I begin
to have need of God's existence.
But if he exists,
in this case
today
more than ever
gradually, I begin to believe
to that holy legend,
that his son
was a simple man like me,
though he could keep
the waves of sea under feet…
Because
how many years,
I'm not only walking,
but I am running
                    on the ocean of
                                        Pain and Love…

* * *

Your the only *Where*
is your name's sadness,
from which you are made:
cheerfully wet,
around your splendid suburb
of neglected,- to the flower
from the death lane‰
the only traveller -
regarding you.

You are coming near, you
don't see him.
He guesses you from
the fever,
that you endeavor your
light's dust
from his pistil to…

But you don't recognize him,
why?
Recognize the «why»!

Earthquake

(Gogyoshi)

Our names are cradles – hanging
From the cold branches of hope.
These days are narcissus –
Deep wounds
In the dream of God.

* * *

The color of ink is the fear of ecstasy
with cold landscape of the night,
from its back it was appeared a sudden hand
between innocence and betrayal$

Whose papers the fingerprints are put on?
with shining after twelve.

The air trembles
like stacked night suit of doubt.

We have to wait
the nudity of dawn...

Cross yourself, Bird!

* * * (Haiku)

The love is a ruin,
where a bird make tinkle
the scar of my ring finger.

* * * (Haiku)

On the skin of the city
are non-healing wounds
people-lotuses.

* * * (Haiku)

Stones – in my prayer.
The silence of God
is an open crack in the air.

* * * (Haiku)

With chapped lips
don't promise love. The word
is a migratory bird.

* * * (Haiku)

My words are
your own presence,
where you are absent.

* * * (Haiku)

You are a stronger
to yourself. The days I lived,
you don't know them.

* * *

I'm the biography of
God's regrets.
he often slipped my destiny's traces.
The water-nymphs' pain
was changed into birds
and pecked the oranges
in my destiny's syllables…

Then God was looking for apples in my palms,
holding with solemn
the repentance ray
and my anniversary was celebrating in that way,
cause
I'm the biography
of God's regrets…

But…
Apples didn't fall from my branchy ribs.
he bequeathed them
to the snake, Eva and Adam
whom he expelled from the Paradise then.
And he forgot to take
some seeds…

Out of paradise
the trajectory of fruit was disappeared
as
the vertical finish of meteorite…

As the angels,
were unable not to forgive God
so
they decided to forget me,
cause I'm the biography
of His regrets...

* * *

There are silences in the sky of the word,
that give the light only at night…

Translated from Armenian by ***Ani Hakobyan***

* * *

Love picks us: we are hanging from the tree of hope
as an empty cradle with non-scarring roses.
There's so much Thomas in my bottomless voice!,
who recognize the light only with their fingers.

Translated from Armenian by ***Nektar Balian-Harutyunyan***

www.ingramcontent.com/pod-product-compliance
Lightning Source LLC
Chambersburg PA
CBHW022202160726
48282CB00024B/300
* 9 7 8 8 1 1 9 2 2 8 5 9 1 *